The Happy House

Written by Jill Eggleton
Illustrated by Philip Webb

T0360100

The people in Harriet's
street did not smile.
They did not look happy.

The cats did not purr.
The dogs did not bark
and the birds did not sing.

3

"I will make a happy house,"
said Harriet.
So Harriet painted
her house purple and green.

She painted a big
yellow sun on the roof
and a big yellow smile
on the door.

Harriet put tables and chairs
in her garden.
She put up blue umbrellas.

She painted big yellow suns
on the umbrellas
and a big yellow smile
on her letterbox.

Harriet put on purple shoes
and a green skirt.
She painted a big
yellow sun on her hat
and a big yellow smile
on her shirt.

She made a sign and put it on her gate...

The people in the street
came to Harriet's house.
Harriet gave them
coffee in blue cups
with yellow smiles.
And they laughed.

The dogs in the street
came to Harriet's house.
Harriet gave them cakes
and they wagged their tails.

The cats in the street
came to Harriet's house.
Harriet gave them cakes
and they purred.

The birds came
to Harriet's house.
They sat on
the blue umbrellas.
Harriet gave them cakes
and they sang.

"Good!" said Harriet.
"There are happy people.
There are happy dogs and
happy cats and happy birds.
This **is** a happy house."

Thank-you Notes

Guide Notes

> **Title: The Happy House**
> **Stage:** Early (2) – Yellow
>
> **Genre:** Fiction
> **Approach:** Guided Reading
> **Processes:** Thinking Critically, Exploring Language, Processing Information
> **Written and Visual Focus:** Thank-you notes
> **Word Count:** 224

THINKING CRITICALLY
(sample questions)
- What do you think this story could be about?
- Focus on the title. What do you think could be meant by a 'Happy House'?
- Why do you think the people in the house were not happy?
- Look at the colours Harriet is using. Why do you think she is choosing yellow, purple and green?
- What do you think made the people, the animals and the birds happy?

EXPLORING LANGUAGE

Terminology
Title, cover, illustrations, author, illustrator

Vocabulary
Interest words: happy, umbrella, purred
High-frequency words (reinforced): the, in, did, not, look, and, I, will, make, house, said, so, her, on, big, put, for, with, they, there, this, is, a
New words: made, people, gave, came, them

Print Conventions
Capital letter for sentence beginnings and names (**H**arriet), full stops, quotation marks, commas, ellipsis